Watches

JUDITH MILLER

MILLER'S

Watches by Judith Miller

First published in Great Britain in 2009 by Miller's,
a division of Mitchell Beazley,
imprints of Octopus Publishing Group Ltd,
2-4 Heron Quays, London E14 4JP.

Miller's is a registered trademark of Octopus Publishing Group Ltd.
An Hachette Livre UK Company.
www.hachettelivre.co.uk

Front cover: tag Heuer Monza Classic watches

UK ISBN 978 184 533 4765
A CIP catalogue record for this book is available from the British Library.

US ISBN 978 1845 334680
                    184533468X
A CIP record for this book is available from the Library of Congress

Distributed in the U.S. and Canada by Octopus Books USA:
c/o Hachette Book Group USA
237 Park Avenue
New York NY 10017

Set in Myriad Pro

Colour reproduction by United Graphics, Singapore
Printed and bound in China by Toppan

Publishing Manager: Julie Brooke
Consultant: Mark Laino
Editor: Sara Sturgess
Sub editors: Katy Armstrong and Daniel Goode
Design: Jeremy Tilston
Indexer: Hilary Bird
Production: Peter Hunt & Lucy Carter

Watches

Contents

Introduction

Over the past few years people have increasingly started to look at watches as more than just a means of telling the time. The trend for men to wear a watch as a fashion accessory has brought new interest to both contemporary and vintage watches by leading makers such as Rolex, Patek Philippe and Audemars Piguet.

Many of these firms began as makers of pocket watches in the 19th century. Developments in technology, and the increasing skills of the watchmakers, enabled them to produce increasingly complex movements.

The number of collectors have fine watches is growing as more and more people appreciate the complexity of the mechanisms, the accuracy of the timekeeping, the many additional functions they contain – from alarms to perpetual calendars – and the quality of the

A Cartier 'St Christopher' Tank Obus watch.

A Volta gold watch, by Maurice Ditisheim.

A Gübelin 'G Quartz' stainless steel wristwatch.

workmanship. On top of this watches remain, for many men, the only piece of "jewellery" it is acceptable to wear.

While very affordable, mass-produced watches have become the ubiquitous, the established, prestigious brands continue to produce handmade watches of exceptional quality. It is these watches which continue to catch the imagination today: made to the highest standards of craftsmanship and from the best materials they are precision instruments we use on a daily basis.

Judith Miller.

1900s

By the turn of the 20th century wristwatches were starting to replace fob or pocket watches as the timepiece of choice for fashionable gentlemen. The Swiss firm Girard-Perregaux and the French jeweller Louis Cartier are credited with making some of the first wristwatches: the former for the German navy and the latter for Brazilian pioneer aviator Alberto Santos-Dumont.

▶ A rare and early French 18ct yellow gold 'Grand Prix - Paris 1900' minute-repeating wristwatch, by Paul Ditisheim, La Chaux-de-Fonds, the movement made for the Paris Exposition Universelle of 1900.
☆☆☆☆☆

> "It is with our judgments as with our watches; no two go just alike, yet each believes his own."
>
> ALEXANDER POPE

▶ A rare and early Swiss Omega silver wristwatch, originally sold in 1905, with left-hand winding mechanism. ☆☆☆

Patek Philippe & Cie.

Founded in 1839 in Geneva, Switzerland, Patek Philippe is well known for its high quality watches, which have been worn by royalty, film stars and tycoons. Some of the most expensive and complicated watches were made for multimillionaire watch collectors: Charles Packard of Warren, Ohio, and Henry Graves Jr. of New York. The latter commissioned what was, at the time, the world's most complicated watch. Work started on the watch functions in 1928, and it took five years to make. In a recent sale at Sotheby's auction house it sold for $11 million (£6.1 million): the highest price ever achieved for a clock or watch.

Wristwatches became desirable during World War II and Patek Philippe responded by producing a range of models designed to be commercial. The range was named Calatrava after the Spanish religious order founded to protect the citadel of Calatrava from Arab invaders. Their ornate cross was used on these watches, and later adopted as the company symbol, now appearing on all Patek Philippe watches. After World War II, the company continued to produce fine-quality wristwatches in conservative-style cases.

Patek Philippe celebrated their 150th anniversary in 1989 by producing a number of limited editions, including just three examples of a piece with 33 functions. This watch was called the Calibre 89 and the yellow gold example sold for $2 million (£1 million).

◀ *An early 1900s Swiss Patek Philippe & Cie, Genève 18ct yellow gold wristwatch, with cushion-shaped case, the strap with 18ct gold Patek Philippe buckle.* ☆☆☆☆

◄ A Tiffany & Co. 18ct gold demi-hunter gentleman's wristwatch, signed on the dial and movement, and the case signed 'TIFFANY & CO 18K', with presentation engraving inside back '1871 Sept 7th 1896'. c1895

▲ A Swiss Patek Philippe & Cie 18ct gold wristwatch, with curved, tonneau-shaped case, the movement made in 1909, cased in 1918. ☆☆☆☆☆

1910s

The second decade of the 20th century saw a host of developments in wristwatch design as more firms began to make their own wristwatches for mass-production. Among them were Longines and Ebel. The demand for practical military watches during World War I led to the creation of protective grilles to cover the watch face hand luminous hands and dials.

▲ A Paul Buhré Taber-type 14ct pink gold large wristwatch, for the Russian market, with single-button chronograph on the crown and register. c1915 ☆☆☆

▶ *A French L. Leroy & Cie 18ct gold wristwatch with day and date calendar. c1910 ☆☆☆*

◀ A Henry Moser & Cie wristwatch, made for the Russian market, with digital days of the week indicator. c1910 ☆☆☆

"Deactivating a generator loop without the correct key is like repairing a watch with a hammer and chisel; one false move and you'll never know the time again."

THE DOCTOR, *DOCTOR WHO*

▲ *An early Swiss Omega silver-cased military wristwatch, with 24-hour dial. c1915* ☆☆☆

Omega

Founded as an assembly workshop in 1848, Omega's first wristwatch was produced in 1900 and was one of the first industrially produced wristwatches.

During World War II, the company produced large numbers of watches for British military officers and airmen. Their post-war designs such as the Seamaster (worn by James Bond in the recent films) and the Constellation were greatly influenced by the requirements of the war: strength and accuracy. The Seamaster and the Constellation were originally self-winding bumper automatics. Omega introduced a range with 360° full rotor, winding automatic movements in 1956. The Speedmaster was created a year later in 1957. In 1965, it was chosen as the official NASA watch, and thereby becoming the first watch on the moon.

By the 1960s Omega had become the brand to own and, as they often produced the same model in 18ct, 14ct or 9ct gold, all price points were covered. The Constellation range was so successful that by 1958 they accounted for 45 per cent of all chronometers sold.

Omega are now one of the most recognised and respected of the watch houses in the world and have often been chosen as the official time keeper for the Olympics, including the 2008 Summer Olympics and the 2010 Winter Olympics.

◀ *A Swiss Omega left-hand winding wristwatch, retailed by Kirby, Beard & Co., Ltd. Paris, sold on January 20, 1910.* ☆☆☆

▼ A Swiss Patek Philippe & Cie 18ct gold and enamel wristwatch, previously owned by Asa Griggs Candler (1851-1929), made in 1919. Candler bought the formula for Coca-Cola from its inventor John Pemberton in 1887 and the success of the brand is largely due to his aggressive marketing.

☆☆☆☆☆☆

◀ *A rare Swiss Patek Philippe & Co., 18ct pink gold large 'Chronometro Gondolo' wristwatch, with curved rectangular case, the strap with 18ct gold buckle bearing London import marks for 1925-26. 1913* ☆☆☆☆☆

Wristwatch development

During World War I the demand for practical watches that were easy to read while struggling through no-man's land or in a muddy trench led to an increase in the number of wristwatch designs. Many of them were little more than a traditional half-hunter pocket watch (watches where the outer cover had an enamelled dial and central glass aperture through which the hands could be read) with additional lugs which could be threaded onto a wrist strap. The dials on these watches did not face the wearer and so they were harder to read and are not as valuable or collectable today. They often had chased or engine-turned decoration on the back, something not seen in purpose-made wristwatches.

Swiss and American makers began to address the need for Trench watches by adding metal grilles to protect the face or by using luminous hands or faces which could be read in the dark. The Swiss – who remained neutral throughout the war – made watches for all sides in the conflict. These are highly sought after today – particularly if they are unworn.

The first British tanks – introduced to the field of battle in 1916 – had a direct effect on watch design, with the Cartier Tank watch developed in 1917. Viewed from above the watch resembles the first tanks.

▶ *A Swiss Rolex silver water-resistant hunting-cased wristwatch, with London import marks for 1916-17.* ☆☆☆

1920s

With the war over, watch design followed the prevailing Art Deco style which influenced everything from architecture to clothing. By 1924 *The Watchmaker (Der Uhrmacher)* magazine reported: "Today it can be said that the wristwatch has conquered the world; it is worn by the woman worker every bit as much as by the society lady; it is particularly popular among the middle classes."

▲ A Swiss Audemars Piguet platinum and blue enamel Art Deco wristwatch, cased and retailed by Charlton & Cie, New York, with tonneau-shaped case. 1920 ☆☆☆☆☆

▶ A Swiss Audemars Piguet 18ct white gold wristwatch, retailed by E. Gubelin, Lucerne, with rectangular Art Deco case, triple-date, age and phases of the moon. 1924 ☆☆☆☆☆

▶ A French Cartier 'St. Christopher' Tank Obus 18ct gold and champleve wristwatch, with square case, special champleve enamel St. Christopher back and Cartier 18ct gold deployant clasp. 1928
☆☆☆☆☆

▶ A French Cartier platinum and 18ct gold large wristwatch, with curved tonneau-shaped case and 18ct white and pink gold 'grains de riz' bracelet with concealed deployant clasp. c1923
☆☆☆☆☆

◀ A French Cartier 18ct gold Art Deco wristwatch, with rare minute-repeating movement in tonneau-shaped case and 'bracelet montre tortue or' registered 1928. This is the first Cartier minute-repeating wristwatch. ✩✩✩✩✩✩

▶ A 1920s French Eberhard & Co. 18ct gold large single-button chronograph, with register, tachometer and telemeter, in fitted case. ✩✩✩

◀ *An Elgin gentleman's wristwatch, with white gold-filled case with fancy-engraved bezel, original dial and ball lugs, with Elgin 15-jewel movement. c1925-26* ☆

"Synchronize your watches. The future's coming back..."

BACK TO THE FUTURE II

▶ A very rare Hamilton 'Piping Rock' gentleman's wristwatch, with 14ct solid white gold case with black enamelled bezel, and early Hamilton 17-jewel movement. c1928 ☆☆☆

38

Harwood automatic watch

The automatic or self-winding watch is a mechanical watch with a mainspring that is wound automatically by the natural motion of the wearer. It dates back to the end of the 18th century, although these automatic pocket watches were produced in very small numbers and had very limited success. Making watches with automatic mechanisms was not attempted again until the 1920s when the wristwatch had replaced the pocket watch in popularity. The new mechanism works much better in this new form because it could charge with the motion of the wearer's arm.

The first automatic wristwatch was made by English watchmaker John Harwood in 1922. He began by using an existing movement and adapted it with his own automatic mechanism. His first model was a round design (opposite), produced in silver, gold and gold plate. The milled-edge bezel was used to set the hands. When fully wound, the watch would run for 12 hours.

Harwood's system used a pivoting weight, which swung as the wearer moved. Spring bumpers limited the weight's swing to approximately 180°: encouraging a back and forth motion. This type of self-winding mechanism is now known as a 'bumper'.

◀ *A Harwood automatic gold-plated wristwatch, the design patented by Englishman John Harwood in 1924. c1926* ☆☆

"When a man retires and time is no longer a matter of urgent importance, his colleagues generally present him with a watch."

R.C. SHERIFF

◄ *A 1920s French Leon Hatot Art Deco 18ct gold and enamel wristwatch, the tonneau-shaped case with hinged cover.* ☆☆☆

A 1920s Danish Jules Jürgensen Art Deco 18ct gold large wristwatch, tortoise-shaped case, the strap with 14ct gold buckle. ☆☆☆☆☆

The case houses a five minute-repeating movement.

▲ A Swiss Longines 18ct gold wristwatch, with single-button chronograph, 100 and 1,000 metres tachometer graduations and register, with an 18ct gold 'grain de riz' bracelet and deployant clasp. c1920 ☆☆☆

"There is time for work. And time for love. That leaves no other time."

COCO CHANEL

◄ A Swiss Longines 18ct gold medical wristwatch, with single-button chronograph, register and pulsometer. c1920

☆☆☆

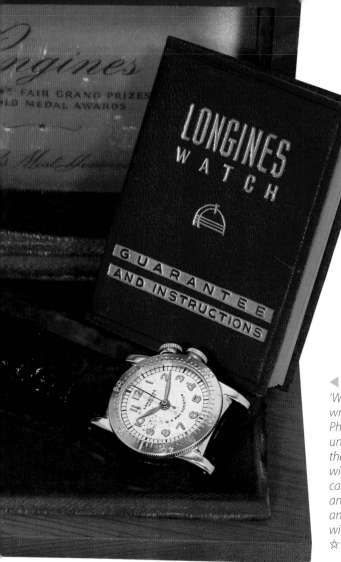

◀ A Swiss Longines 'Weems' steel aviators' wristwatch, invented by Philip Van Horn Weems under US Pat. 2008734, the stainless steel case with rotating calibrated bezel, and with hour-angle and centre-seconds, with fitted case. c1925 ☆☆

▶ A 1920s Swiss
Niton 18ct gold
wristwatch, with
rectangular case
and jump-hour
movement.
☆☆☆☆☆

▶ A Swiss Patek Philippe & Cie 18ct gold drivers' wristwatch, with rectangular horizontal case, the strap with 18ct gold Patek Philippe buckle. 1920 ☆☆☆☆☆

◀ A Swiss Omega oversized silver military wristwatch, with box. c1925 ☆☆☆☆

48

◀ A Swiss Patek Philippe & Cie 18ct gold wristwatch, with single-button chronograph on the crown, luminous dial with vertical register, tachometer, the strap with 18ct gold Patek Philippe buckle. 1927 ☆☆☆☆☆☆

▲ A Swiss Patek Philippe & Cie 18ct pink gold wristwatch, with square case, the strap with 18ct pink gold Patek Philippe buckle. 1928 ☆☆☆

Rolex

Rolex is the largest luxury watch brand, producing about 2,000 watches per day. The company (known as Wilsdorf & Davis) was founded in London in 1903. The trademark 'Rolex' was registered in 1908 and officially adopted as the company name in 1915. Rolex moved to Switzerland in 1919 as British taxes and export duties on gold and silver were driving costs up.

The company made no attempt to enter the automatic wristwatch market until 1929 when Harwood (see p39) went bankrupt – until then the company's many patents had prevented or restricted other companies from creating automatic watches. Rolex had designed the waterproof Oyster case in 1927 and in the early 1930s they designed a silent 360° self-winding movement. Unfortunately the motor was very large, so these watches had domed case backs which became known as 'Bubble Backs'. The Bubble Back was launched in 1934.

In the 1950s diving became a popular sport. Rolex realised the importance of being able to measure time under water and designed one of its most famous watches: the Submariner. Early models of the Submariner are known as 'James Bond' watches because an example was worn by the eponymous hero in the first four films.

Rolex SA currently has three watch lines: Oyster Perpetual, Professional and Cellini. From 1946, Rolex has sold less expensive watches under the brand name, 'Tudor'. American sales of this line were discontinued in 2004.

◀ *1920s Swiss Rolex sterling silver mid-sized wristwatch, with early water-resistant double-case and Prima movement.* ☆☆

▶ *A 1920s Swiss Rolex 18ct gold wristwatch, with narrow, curved rectangular water-resistant case, with London import marks for 1926.* ☆☆☆ .

► *A late 1920s Swiss Rolex Oyster 18ct gold chronometer wristwatch, with water-resistant, octagonal case.*
☆☆☆

▲ A late 1920s Swiss Rolex Oyster Majestic Observatory 9ct gold wristwatch, ref. 679, with water-resistant octagonal case and centre-seconds. ☆☆☆

▶ A 1920s Swiss Rolex 9ct gold wristwatch, with water-resistant cushion-shaped case, the strap with 18ct gold Rolex buckle, watch with Glasgow import marks for 1929. ☆☆☆

◀ A Swiss Vacheron & Constantin 18ct white and yellow gold Art Deco wristwatch, Verger Frères Paris, the dial concealed by shutters, with two crowns, the strap with 18ct gold buckle. 1928
☆☆☆☆☆

▲ A Swiss Vacheron & Constantin 18ct gold and platinum wristwatch, the rectangular case with concealed dial, the strap with yellow gold Vacheron & Constantin buckle. 1929
☆☆☆☆☆☆

◀ A Swiss Vacheron & Constantin platinum wristwatch, with curved rectangular case, the strap with later 18ct white gold buckle, together with Vacheron & Constantin case. 1929 ☆☆☆☆

"Three witches watch three wristwatches, which witch watches which wristwatch?"

TONGUE TWISTER

▶ A 1920s French Volta 18ct gold large wristwatch, made by Maurice Ditisheim, with minute-repeating mechanism and 18ct gold textured mesh bracelet. ☆☆☆☆

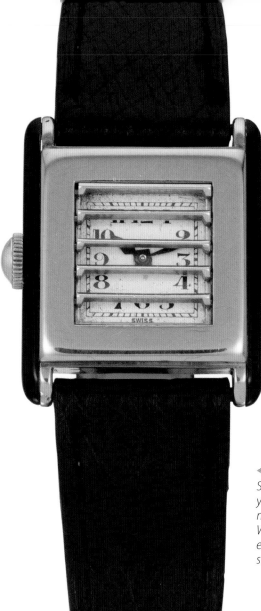

◀ *A 1920s Verger France, Ste S.G.D.G. 18ct white and yellow gold wristwatch, the movement signed 'Camy Watch Co', the black enamel outer case with shutters.* ☆☆☆

◀ *A 1920s French Art Deco 18ct white and yellow gold wristwatch, made by R.B., the case set with diamonds, the strap with pink gold deployant clasp.* ☆☆

1930s

The popularity of wristwatches continued to grow in the period leading up to World War II as manufacturers capitalised on the new Art Deco style. New developments included waterproof and automatic watches as well as those designed for a particular activity such as the Jaeger-LeCoultre Reverso for sportsmen.

▶ *A 1930s ATO Rolls nickel-chromium wristwatch, by Leon Hatot, the rectangular case with self-winding mechanism.* ☆☆

◀ *A 1930s Swiss Henri Blanc silver Art Deco wristwatch, with jump-hour indicator and rectangular case.*
☆☆☆

▶ A 1930s Bulova gentleman's wristwatch, with elongated gold-filled case, champagne dial with blue steel hands, and 17-jewel movement. This watch is hard to find in this case as it was deemed too long in its day, and few were sold. The movement is one used in a lady's watch because the thinness of the case requires a similarly thin and small movement. ☆

A 1930s French Cartier 'Tank Americaine' 18ct gold large wristwatch, with curved rectangular case, the strap with 18ct gold Cartier deployant clasp.
☆☆☆☆☆

◄ *A 1930s French Cartier 'Duo-Plan' 18ct gold wristwatch, with rectangular case, the strap with 18ct pink gold Cartier deployant clasp.*
✫✫✫

> *"There are people whose watch stops at a certain hour and who remain permanently at that age."*
>
> SAINTE-BEAVE

▲ *A desirable 1930s Elgin manual wind gentleman's wristwatch, with white gold-filled case with stepped bezel, and 15-jewel movement, in excellent condition.* ☆

◀ *A 1930s Elgin gentleman's wristwatch, with solid 14ct white gold case with engraved and enamelled bezel with stylised floral pattern, the white face with luminous hands and numbers and subsidiary seconds dial at six o'clock, and 17-jewel movement.* ☆

"Time is our most valuable asset, yet we tend to waste it, kill it and spend it rather than invest it."

JIM ROHN

▶ A 1930s Elgin gentleman's wristwatch, with 'cut corner' white 14ct gold case, 15-jewel movement, seconds dial at 6 o'clock, and luminous dial and hands. ☆

▶ *Hamilton 'Stanley' gentleman's wristwatch, with yellow gold-filled case, solid gold applied numbers and subsidiary seconds dial at six o'clock, and with Hamilton 401 17-jewel movement. The 401 is the rarest of Hamilton's movements and only a few of the desirable Stanley models were fitted with it. c1931 ☆*

◄ A 1930s Hamilton Art Deco gentleman's wristwatch, with platinum rectangular case with hooded barrel lugs, diamond markers and Hamilton 980 17-jewel movement. The hooded barrel lugs are a typical feature of 1930s watches. ☆☆☆

Hamilton Watch Company

The Hamilton Watch Company was founded in Lancaster, Pennsylvania in 1892. Its stated objective "was to build only watches of the highest quality".

During the 1910s, Hamilton became supplier to the US Armed Forces. The first of these wristwatches were used by General "Black Jack" Pershing and his troops who were fighting in the European trenches. During World War II, Hamilton stopped production of watches for consumers so it could concentrate on the production of one million timepieces for the army. The Hamilton marine chronometer was the first to be produced by modern manufacturing methods. Approximately 10,000 Hamilton marine chronometers were worn by US troops in World War II.

The firm continued to produce watches on an industrial scale after the war, with models created to appeal across the market. Its watches had a reputation for reliability and were supplied to railway companies.

The world's first electric (battery-powered) watch, the Ventura, was introduced by Hamilton in 1957. The Ventura was worn by Elvis Presley in 'Blue Hawaii' in 1961, and, more recently, by Will Smith in the 'Men in Black' films.

Hamilton also created the world's first digital watch, which started measuring time at 12.01 New York Time on 6th May 1970.

◀ *A 1930s Hamilton 'Brook' gentleman's wristwatch, with shaped gold-filled case, and 17-jewel movement. This is an early first model driver's watch, with the case shaped to fit the side of the wrist.* ☆

▶ A 1930s Illinois 'Mate' gentleman's wristwatch, with white gold-filled case with chevron-engraved bezel, the two-tone dial with luminous hands and numbers and subsidiary seconds dial at nine o'clock, and with 17-jewel movement. ☆

▶ *A 1930s Swiss Jaeger-LeCoultre 'Reverso' stainless steel 'Staybrite' wristwatch, with curved rectangular reversable case.*
☆☆☆

"I've been on a calendar, but I have never been on time."

MARILYN MONROE

▶ *A top of the range 1930s Art Deco Longines wristwatch, with platinum case and diamond-set dial, Longines 17-jewel movement, seconds subdial at 6 o'clock.* ☆☆☆

A 1930 Swiss Longines 14ct gold wristwatch, with curved rectangular case. ☆☆☆

▲ A 1930s Swiss Longines 'Lindbergh' 10ct gold-filled aviators' wristwatch, invented by Col. Chas. A. Lindbergh, with hour angle, indirect centre-seconds and two crowns.
☆☆☆☆☆

▶ A Swiss Longines stainless steel large military wristwatch, manufactured for the British Ministry of Defence, with anti-magnetic, water-resistant case, centre-seconds and Ministry of Defence 'broad arrow' marks. c1939 ☆☆☆

▶ *A 1930s Swiss Omega large stainless steel 'Staybrite' wristwatch.* ☆☆☆

▶ A Swiss Omega 'pupitre' stainless steel 'Staybrite' wristwatch, with rectangular case, the strap with stainless steel Omega buckle. c1938 ☆☆☆

Art Deco Style

The geometric styling associated with the Art Deco movement can be seen in many watches of the period. Rectangular cases became extremely popular in the 1920s and '30s and as a consequence the demand for circular models wained until the 1950s. However, the shape of chronographs, which were used for activities such as driving, flying and sports in general, remained circular in the main.

Typical Art Deco embellishments include enamelled bezels (visible on the Hamilton Coronado and Piping Rock models), sword-shaped hands, a flat crown, and diamond-set cocktail watches for ladies.

The Art Deco style was influenced by new advances in travel, with air travel and the motor car becoming more easily available to those who could afford them. Among the novelties on offer were watches based on car radiator designs. These were probably worn by car owners. The Swiss firm Mido, founded in 1918, pioneered these watches, such as the Bugatti, which imitated the car's horseshoe-shaped radiator and featured the same red oval enamel plaque with the Bugatti logo, and a winding button at 12 o'clock imitating the car's filler cap. Only 20 of these watches are believed to have been produced and are therefore one of the rarest models ever made and can be worth up to £35,000 each. Mido also created watches based on Chevrolet and Fiat cars, amongst others.

◀ *1930s Patek Philippe & Cie Art Deco 18ct white gold wristwatch, with thin, rectangular case, the strap with 18ct white gold Patek Philippe buckle.* ☆☆☆☆☆

▶ *A Swiss Patek Philippe & Cie 'Calatrava' stainless steel 'Staybrite' wristwatch. 1938*
☆☆☆☆

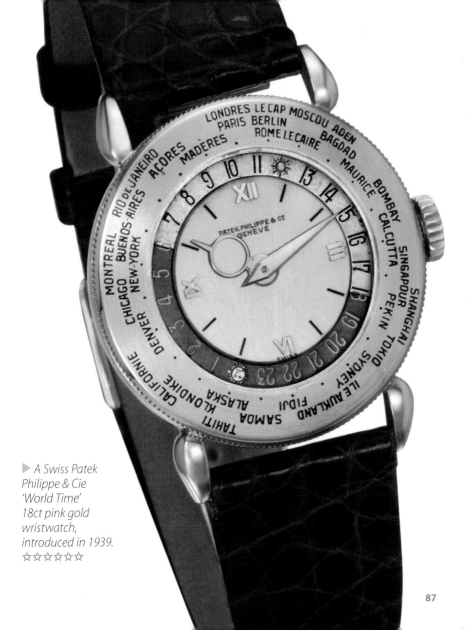

▶ A Swiss Patek
Philippe & Cie
'World Time'
18ct pink gold
wristwatch,
introduced in 1939.
☆☆☆☆☆☆

◀ *A 1930s Swiss Rolex Oyster Perpetual 'Rigid Hooded' stainless steel and gold chronometer wristwatch, with tonneau-shaped, water-resistant case and self-winding movement.* ☆☆☆

▶ *A 1930s Swiss Rolex Oyster stainless steel chronograph wristwatch, with tonneau-shaped water-resistant case, round-button chronograph, registers, tachometer and telemeter.* ☆☆☆☆☆

▶ A 1930s Swiss Rolex 18ct gold wristwatch, with curved rectangular case and 18ct gold link bracelet.
☆☆☆☆

▶ *A 1930s Swiss Rolex 'Dauphin' stainless steel and 18ct pink gold wristwatch, with rectangular case.* ☆☆☆

▶ *A 1930s Swiss Rolex 'Prince Classic' stainless steel and 9ct gold chronometer wristwatch, with duo-dial, the strap with gold-plated Rolex buckle.*
☆☆☆☆

"*I don't wear a watch. I want my arms to weigh the same.*"

HARRY HILL

▶ *A 1930s Swiss Rolex stainless steel 'digital' wristwatch, with curved rectangular case, jump-hour, the bracelet with Rolex clasp.*
☆☆☆☆☆

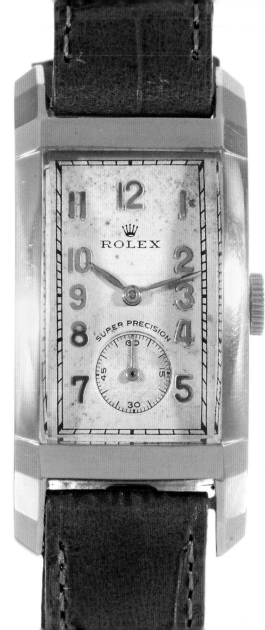

◀ *A 1930s Swiss Rolex 'Elegant' stainless steel wristwatch, the strap with stainless steel Rolex buckle.* ✩✩✩✩

▶ *A Swiss Rolex anti-magnetic stainless steel wristwatch, with square case and square-button chronograph and register. c1939* ✩✩✩✩✩

◀ A 1930s Art Deco platinum wristwatch, made by C.H. Meylan, Le Brassus for Tiffany & Co., with rectangular case.
☆☆☆

"Time is the old justice
that examines all
such offenders."

WILLIAM SHAKESPEARE

▶ A 1930s Swiss
Tissot stainless steel
wristwatch, with
olive-shaped-button
chronograph and
register. ☆☆☆☆

◀ *A 1930s Tissot stainless steel 'Staybrite' large chronograph wristwatch, with claw lugs, oval single-button chronograph, register, tachometer, telemeter and black dial.* ☆☆☆☆

▲ *A Swiss Vacheron & Constantin stainless steel 'Staybrite' timekeeper wristwatch, with two complications, single-button chronograph, register and tachometer. 1935* ☆☆☆☆☆☆

> *"Time is an illusion. Lunchtime doubly so."*
>
> DOUGLAS ADAMS

▲ *A Swiss Vacheron & Constantin stainless steel wristwatch, with winding crown at 12 o'clock. 1936*
☆☆☆

▶ A 1930s Waltham gentleman's wristwatch, with 14ct white gold 'Solidarity' case with highly engraved bezel, silvered dial with subsidiary seconds dial at six o'clock, and matching 'Solidarity' engraved solid 14ct white gold buckle. ☆

1940s

Manufacturers in Europe and the US made watches for the military throughout World War II influencing the design of civilian watches which, as a result, became larger and more masculine. The Swiss, who remained neutral throughout the conflict, also made military watches but were free to develop new technology such as a perpetual calendar and a wristwatch alarm.

◀ A Swiss
Audemars
Piguet 18ct gold
astronomic
wristwatch,
with triple-date,
lunar calendar
and moon
phases. c1949
☆☆☆☆☆

◀ A 1940s Bailey Banks & Biddle wristwatch, with platinum case, hooded lugs, diamond-set dial and Swiss-made 27-jewel movement, the back stamped 'PLATINUM'. High end jewellery retailer Bailey Banks & Biddle were founded in Philadelphia in 1832 and now have over 70 stores in 24 US states. This watch would have been made for them in Switzerland under contract, and marked with their name. ☆☆☆

"Dogs lead a nice life. You never see a dog with a wristwatch."

GEORGE CARLIN

▶ *A 1940s Bulova gentleman's wristwatch with 14ct solid pink gold rectangular case, silvered dial and Bulova 21-jewel movement. Bulova produced a large number of watches in pink gold during this period.* ☆

> *"We must use time as a tool, not as a crutch."*
>
> JOHN F. KENNEDY

◀ *A 1940s French Cartier 'Moneta' 18ct gold wristwatch.* ☆☆☆

Cartier

Louis-François Cartier founded Cartier in Paris in 1847, after taking over the workshop of his master, Adolphe Picard. Focusing almost entirely on jewellery, the company quickly became a favourite of the Imperial court. It was Louis-Francois's grandsons, Louis, Pierre and Jacques, who were responsible for establishing the worldwide brand name.

In 1904, Brazilian aviator Alberto Santos-Dumont complained to his friend Louis Cartier of the impracticality of using a pocket watch whilst flying. With the help of master watchmaker Edmond Jaeger, Cartier designed a flat wristwatch (called the Santos) with a distinctive square bezel for his friend. The Santos was the first men's wristwatch and was put into commercial production seven years later and is still made today.

Louis was also responsible for the design of the famous 'Tank' watch in 1917. It was named after, and said to be inspired by, the tanks, which had helped to bring World War I to a close. This rectangular watch pioneered 'sword' hands and 'railway tracks' to show minutes and it is now one of the most popular and recognised watch designs ever. Over thirty variations are currently produced by Cartier Monde.

◀ *A 1940s French Cartier 18ct pink gold large 'Tank' wristwatch, the 18ct pink gold 'a mailles' bracelet with concealed deployant clasp, with fitted box.* ☆☆☆☆☆

▶ *A 1940s Swiss Eberhard & Co. stainless steel 'Staybrite' large chronograph wristwatch, with square-button chronograph, register, tachometer and telemeter.* ☆☆☆

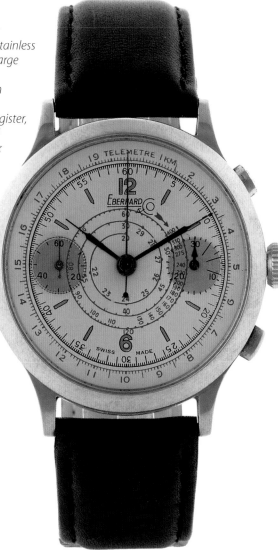

"Let's sympathise our watches!"

THE THREE STOOGES

▶ A 1940s Gruen Curvex
Precision 10ct gold filled
gentleman's wristwatch with
rectangular-shaped case,
signed on the case,
movement, dial and crown,
with 17-jewel movement.
The inset lines were once
enamelled, as indicated by the
remains of the enamel on the
bottom of the case. ☆

◀ A Hamilton 'Endicott' gentleman's wristwatch, with 10ct gold-filled case, the two-tone silvered dial with Roman numerals. A version with a subsidiary seconds dial at six o'clock was also produced, and one with gold-filled Arabic numerals, both variations are shown on the watch to the right. c1941 ☆

◀ *A Hamilton 'Gilbert' gentleman's wristwatch, with 14ct solid gold rectangular case, dial with applied solid gold numbers and subsidiary seconds dial at six o'clock, and Hamilton 982 19-jewel movement. c1941* ☆

▲ A Swiss International Watch Co. stainless steel oversized military pilot's wristwatch, from a limited series of 1,000 for the German Air Force, with anti-magnetic and anti-corrosion case, indirect seconds and original IWC aviator's leather strap. 1940 ☆☆☆☆☆

◀ An early 1940s Swiss Jaeger-LeCoultre nickle-plated RAF military wristwatch, with water-resistant case. ☆☆☆

▶ A 1940s LeCoultre gentleman's chronograph wristwatch, triple-signed on the case, dial and movement, with stainless steel case, original dial with overlapping pulsations, and LeCoultre 17-jewel movement. ☆☆

◀ *A 1940s German Laco-Durowe matte nickle-plated bronze large military aviator's stop-wristwatch, produced by Lacher & Co., with indirect centre-seconds and Guillaume balance.*
☆☆☆

◀ A 1940s Swiss Liban gold-filled chronograph, with 17-jewel 'Venus' movement, and stainless steel back. Venus was one of the few chronograph makers – all are owned by Swatch today. ☆

▲ A Swiss Longines 'Hydrographic Survey' sterling silver military diver's wristwatch, made for the British Royal Navy, with special water-resistant winding cover and centre-seconds. c1942 ☆☆☆☆☆

"Half our life is spent trying to find something to do with the time we have rushed through life trying to save."

WILL ROGERS

▶ A 1940s May's gentleman's wristwatch, with 14ct solid pink gold square case and Swiss-made 17-jewel movement. Mays is the parent company of Macey's department store. This watch was made and assembled in Switzerland and the dial was customised with the client's name. ☆

▶ A 1940s Movado gentleman's chronograph wristwatch, with 18ct solid gold case, and 17-jewel movement, signed on the case, dial and movement. The presence of pulsations at the end of a time period and the additional registers may indicate that this was an aviator's watch. ☆☆☆

Military watches

Ranging from grill-covered watches produced by Omega in World War I to the Hamilton watches produced in America for the US military in World War II. Military watches are collected as pieces of history.

The wristwatch proved so practical in WWI, that by WWII both sides wanted large volumes of watches that were easy to use, economic and able to withstand the rigours of combat. Many features we now take for granted, like anti-magnetic movements, were invented in this period and these developments were adopted so readily by the general market that there is now no concrete definition of a military watch; only the very rarest watches have been reserved solely for military use. It can confidently be stated that the two World Wars cemented the popularity of the wristwatch.

Military watches were sometimes customised to meet government specifications – an example being the white dial IWC Mark XIs modified by the British Ministry of Defence. These are very rare and highly desirable as a result. Most military watches sell for less than £1,000, but the more unusual, customised examples, can command more, such as the Rolex Submariner which sold in 2002 for £9,000 ($16,000).

The most desirable examples are those that have clear marks of provenance, such as a British government arrow.

◀ *A Rolex/Officine Panerai stainless steel 'Radiomir Panerai' large military diver's wristwatch, first generation made for Italian Navy Commandos, with water-resistant, cushion-shaped case, the strap with Panerai buckle. c1940* ☆☆☆☆☆

◀ A Swiss Omega stainless steel aviator's wristwatch, made for the British Military, with water-resistant case. 1944 ☆☆☆

▶ A Swiss Omega 14ct gold 'bumper' wristwatch, with square case, centre-seconds, self-winding 'bumper' movement, the strap with gold-plated Omega buckle. 1947 ☆☆☆

▶ *A Swiss Omega 18ct gold 'Centenary' chronograph wristwatch, with self-winding mechanism, the strap with gold-plated Omega buckle. Made to commemorate Omega's centenary. 1948 ☆☆☆*

> "Either this man is dead or my watch has stopped."
>
> GROUCHO MARX

▶ A Swiss Patek Philippe & Cie 18ct pink gold 'top hat' wristwatch, with rectangular bombé case. 1942
☆☆☆☆

▼ *A Swiss Patek Philippe & Cie stainless steel military-type wristwatch, the water-resistant case with luminous dial and hands. 1944* ☆☆☆☆☆

▲ *A Swiss Patek Philippe & Cie 18ct pink and white gold driver's wristwatch. c1940*
☆☆☆☆☆

◄ A Swiss Patek Philippe & Cie 18ct gold first series perpetual-chronograph wristwatch, with perpetual calendar, moon phases, square-button chronograph, register and tachometer, the strap with 18ct yellow gold Patek Philippe buckle. c1948

☆☆☆☆☆☆

◀ ▶ *A Rolex 'Bubble Back' wristwatch, with 14ct solid gold case, 18-jewel automatic movement, reference no. 3131. The reference number and the raised 'bubble back' allow this watch to be dated to around 1942-45.* ☆☆☆

▶ *A 1940s Swiss Rolex 'Prince' stainless steel and pink gold wristwatch, with curved rectangular case and two-tone dial, the strap with stainless steel Rolex buckle.* ☆☆

▶ A late 1940s Rolex Oyster anti-magnetic stainless steel chronograph wristwatch, with water-resistant case, round-button chronograph, registers and triple-date calendar, the strap with stainless steel Rolex buckle.
☆☆☆☆☆

"I do not object to people looking at their watches when I am speaking. But I strongly object when they start shaking them to make sure they are still going."

WILLIAM NORMAN BIRKETT,
1ST BARON BIRKETT

▶ A Swiss Vacheron & Constantin 18ct pink gold large wristwatch, with square case, centre-seconds and self-winding mechanism, the strap with 18ct pink gold Vacheron & Constantin buckle. 1948
☆☆☆☆☆

1950s

The sense of optimism felt around the world was less apparent in the wristwatch industry where prices remained relatively high. While many aspired to owning a watch, only the well-heeled could generally afford one. Designs remained simple, with small circular faces and automatic watches being popular. However, innovations included the first battery-driven watch.

> *"The time is always right to do what is right."*
>
> MARTIN LUTHER KING, JR.

▲ *A 1950s Swiss Audemars Piguet gentleman's wristwatch, with 18ct solid gold case with two-tone white and yellow gold bezel, ultra-thin 17 jewel movement with four adjustments, and signed on the dial, case and movement.*
☆☆☆

◀ A 1950s Benrus 10ct gold-filled 'bottle cap' gentleman's watch, numbered 545697, with 21-jewel movement. The leaf logo under the name indicates the company's best 21-jewel movement is inside. Standard movements have 15-17 jewels. This case takes its name from the inspiration behind it: a bottle cap. ☆

◀ A 1950s Benrus 'Jump-Hour' gentleman's wristwatch, with gold-filled waterproof case, hour and minutes apertures, and Benrus 17-jewel movement. This model was top of the range at the time, and was also the company's 'dressiest' design. ☆

◀ *A French Breguet type XX stainless steel military chronograph wristwatch, with water-resistant case and round button 'retour en vol' chronograph and register. c1956* ☆☆☆

◀ A 1950s Swiss Breiting 18ct pink gold large wristwatch, with rectangular-button chronograph, registers, date function and moon phase, the strap with gold-plated Breitling buckle.
☆☆☆

◀ ▶ *Bulova 'Photo' or 'Flip Up' gentleman's wristwatch, with catch to base of dial case to release the sprung flap, signed four times on the case, dial, movement and crown, with 10ct gold-filled case and 21-jewel Swiss-made Bulova movement. The 'L0' marking on the back means this was made in 1950. Despite the fact that the watch itself is very ordinary, this model is sought after, with many buyers placing photographs of loved ones under the flip cover.* ☆

"You know what my father went through to git me that watch? I don't wanna get into it right now, but he went through a lot."

BRUCE, *PULP FICTION*

◀ *A 1950s Bulova gentleman's wristwatch, with 14ct white solid gold rectangular case with bell lugs, the black dial with subsidiary seconds dial and magnifying curved crystal, with Bulova 21-jewel movement.* ☆

◀ A 1950s Lord Elgin gentleman's wristwatch, with a gold-filled bevelled case and matching articulated strap, the dial with fancy numbers, and with a 21-jewel Lord Elgin movement. ☆

◀ A 1950s Lord Elgin Shockmaster 'Stingray' gentleman's wristwatch, with yellow gold-filled shaped case, dial with horizontal lines and subsidiary seconds dial and 21-jewel movement. The Elgin version has a 19-jewel movement. ☆

"Oh! Do not attack me with your watch. A watch is always too fast or too slow. I cannot be dictated to by a watch."

JANE AUSTEN

◀ *A 1950s Lord Elgin 'mystery' wristwatch, with gold-filled case, the revolving inner disc being the hour hand, the outer disc the minute hand, the arrow-heads marking the time, with Lord Elgin 21-jewel movement.* ☆

▶ A 1950s Gruen gentleman's wristwatch, signed four times on the case, movement, dial and crown, with 14ct solid gold case, pink dial and 17-jewel movement. Even though the pink face is more desirable, much of the value of this watch is in the gold case. ☆

◀ A 1950s Gruen 'Continental' gentleman's wristwatch, with 14ct solid white gold case with saucer bezel, black face, and Gruen-signed 17-jewel manual movement. ☆

▶ *A 1950s Hamilton 'Electric Titan' gentleman's wristwatch, signed four times on the dial, case, movement and crown, with 10ct gold-filled stepped bezel and flared lugs and Hamilton 505 battery-powered movement. This was Hamilton's first battery-powered watch and was a commercial failure as the movement was so hard to repair. Surprisingly, replacement batteries are still available today.* ☆

"Time is a companion that goes with us on a journey. It reminds us to cherish each moment, because it will never come again. What we leave behind is not as important as how we have lived."

CAPTAIN JEAN-LUC PICARD,
STAR TREK: GENERATIONS

▶ *A 1950s Hamilton 'Tyrone' gentleman's wristwatch, with 10ct gold-filled bezel with stainless steel back, seconds subsidiary dial at six o'clock, and Hamilton 17-jewel movement, signed Tyrone on inside of case back.* ☆

▶ A 1950s Swiss International Watch Co. 18ct pink gold wristwatch, with centre-seconds, the strap with 18ct pink gold IWC buckle. ✩✩✩

◀ *A Swiss Jaeger-LeCoultre stainless steel wristwatch, with water-resistant case, self-winding mechanism, centre-seconds and power-reserve indicator. c1951* ☆☆

"He is winding the watch of his wit; by and by it will strike."

WILLIAM SHAKESPEARE

Automatic watches

The challenge of creating an automatic, or self-winding watch has intrigued watchmakers since the late 18th century. Early attempts involved a winding weight similar to a pedometer and a rotor moving through 360°. The English watchmaker John Harwood *(see pp38–39)* created the first automatic watch in 1922, but the idea was not taken up by other manufacturers and this, combined with the Wall Street Crash and technical difficulties, meant development went no further.

The Swiss firm Eterna launched an automatic watch in 1938. Ten years later its Eterna-matic model featured an automatic winding mechanism where the rotor axle was fitted with five ball bearings – a motif based on these ball bearings is still used on Eterna watch faces today. Automatic watches became particularly popular during the 1950s – a trend that has continued throughout the succeeding decades.

Patek Philippe's modern day automatic watches feature a 22ct gold winding rotor and are said to be the nearest thing to a handmade watch. Collectable automatic watches are also made by IWC, Jaeger-LeCoultre, Omega and Rolex.

◀ *A 1950s Jaeger-LeCoultre 'Memovox' gentleman's alarm wristwatch, with stainless steel case and 17-jewel movement with VXN markings. The movement is very desirable as it bears markings for the high quality maker Vacheron. Steel is also rarer than gold-filled, as it was more expensive when it was made. The Memovox range and alarm wristwatches in general, are currently very popular. The central dial is moved to set the time for the alarm, indicated by the arrow-head. ☆ ☆*

◀ *A 1950s LeCoultre automatic wristwatch, with 18ct solid gold case with rare 'hobnail' bezel, and 17-jewel Swiss full 'toro' automatic movement.* ☆☆

◀ *A 1950s Swiss Jaeger-LeCoultre 18ct pink gold Futurematic wristwatch, with self-winding mechanism, 40-hour power reserve and back-winder.* ☆☆☆

◀ *A 1950s Swiss Jaeger LeCoultre stainless steel triple wristwatch, with triple-date calendar and moon phases.*
☆☆☆

◀ *A 1950s Junghans gentleman's wristwatch, with asymetrical gold-filled case, and 17-jewel movement.* ☆

"Time: that which man is always trying to kill, ends in killing him."

HERBERT SPENSER

◀ A late 50s or early 60s Swiss Jules Jurgensen gentleman's wristwatch, with square solid 14ct gold case, and signed Jules Jurgensen 17-jewel manual-wind movement. ☆

◀ A 1950s Longines gentleman's wristwatch, with 14ct solid yellow gold rectangular case, diamond dial and Longines 17-jewel movement. ☆☆

"Even if your watch is full of diamonds the hour is still 60 minutes."

ROBERT FULGHUM

▶ *A 1950s Longines gentleman's wristwatch, with solid platinum rectangular case, black dial set with diamonds, and Longines 17-jewel movement.* ☆☆

"*If all time is eternally present All time is unredeemable.*"

T.S. ELIOT

▶ *A 1950s Longines gentleman's wristwatch, with 14ct solid gold case with applied fancy stepped lugs, diamond dial, and Longines 17-jewel movement.*
☆☆

 ▶ A 1950s Swiss Movado gentleman's wristwatch, with a Zenith 17-jewel manual-wind movement and gold-filled case. ☆

▶ A 1950s Movado 'Kingmatic' gentleman's wristwatch, with stainless steel case, the silvered face with day and date apertures, and 28-jewel movement. The back is stamped 'SUB-SEA' indicating it is waterproof. ☆

▶ *A 1950s Swiss Movado 18ct pink gold wristwatch, with self-winding mechanism.* ☆

▶ *A Swiss Omega 18ct gold chronometer wristwatch, with self-winding mechanism. c1950* ☆☆☆

▲ A Swiss Omega stainless steel 'Staybrite' Seamaster wristwatch, with water-resistant case, centre-seconds and stainless steel link bracelet. c1958 ☆☆☆

▶ A late 1950s Swiss Omega stainless steel and gold officially certified chromometer Constellation wristwatch, with water-resistant case, centre-seconds and self-winding mechanism, the strap with Omega buckle. ☆☆☆

▶ *A 1950s Rolex 'Air King' Oyster Perpetual automatic gentleman's wristwatch, with brushed stainless steel case and band, and signed 'Rolex', 26-jewel full rotor movement. The Air King sits at the lower end of the Rolex range, but is still of excellent quality.* ☆☆

◀ *A Swiss Patek Philippe & Cie 18ct white gold wristwatch, the dial with diamond indexes, self-winding mechanism, water-resistant case and 18ct white gold brick-link chain. 1956* ☆☆☆☆☆

◀ *A 1950s Swiss Rolex anti-magnetic 18ct gold oversized chronograph wristwatch, with coin-edge case, square-button chronograph, register, tachometer and telemeter.* ☆☆☆☆☆

▲ *A Rolex Oyster anti-magnetic stainless steel chronograph wristwatch, with water-resistant case, round-button chronograph, registers and triple-date calendar, the strap with stainless steel Rolex buckle.* ☆☆☆☆☆

Vacheron-Constantin

The genesis of the Vacheron-Constantin company occurred in 1755 when Jean-Marc Vacheron founded his own watch-making workshop in Geneva and quickly gained a reputation for high quality work. In 1785 Vacheron's son, Abraham took the helm and he in turn was succeeded by his son, Jacques-Barthélemy in 1810, who began exporting to France and Italy.

The company's slogan – 'Faire Mieux si possible, ce qui est toujours possible' (Do better if possible and that is always possible) – was coined in 1819 when Francois Constantin joined the company and it became Vacheron & Constantin. Constantin travelled the world to market the company's watches, opening new markets, particularly in America. The name 'Vacheron & Constantin, Fabricants, Geneve' was adopted officially in 1877 and did not change again until the mid-1970s when the '&' was dropped and the company became 'Vacheron-Constantin'.

The company produced its first wristwatch in 1928. Other 20th century innovations included a watch named Patrimony in 1955. Billed as the world's thinnest watch it was only 5.25mm thick. Vacheron-Constantin is credited by many with having made the world's most expensive wristwatch – the Kallista. When it was made in 1979 its initial price was $5 million. Today, however, the watch is valued at about $11 million. The Kallista had 118 emerald-cut diamonds, took about 6,000 hours to make, followed by about 20 months for the jewels to be added.

◀ *A Swiss Vacheron & Constantin minute-repeating 18ct gold large wristwatch, with extra-flat case. 1952* ☆☆☆☆☆

▶ *A 1950s Swiss Zenith 18ct gold wristwatch, with square-button chronograph, register and tachometer.*
☆☆☆

◀ *A Swiss Vacheron & Constantin platinum and diamond wristwatch, with flared rectangular case, the strap with white gold Vacheron buckle. 1953*
☆☆☆☆☆

1960s

The social changes witnessed throughout society in the Sixties also impacted on watch design. Larger models weren't reserved for men and could be worn by both sexes. Firms such as Piaget set dials with coloured stones and diamonds, while others, notably Patek Philippe, pushed the boundaries with asymmetrical faces. The development of battery-powered watches continued, with both Swiss and Japanese prototypes launched in 1969.

▶ A 1960s Audemars Piguet 18ct gold skeletonized mid-sized wristwatch, the strap with 18ct gold Audemars buckle.
☆☆☆

> "When a guy takes off his coat, he's not going to fight. When a guy takes off his wristwatch, watch out!"
>
> AL MCGUIRE

▲ A 1960 Swiss Audemars Piguet 18ct white gold wristwatch, with very thin case, the strap with 18ct gold Audemars buckle. ☆☆☆

▶ A 1960s Baume & Mercier 'Traction Avant' 18ct pink and white gold wristwatch, the case in the form of a stylized Citroen Traction Avant, with two diamonds as headlights and a ruby as a rear light.
☆☆☆

▶ A Swiss Breitling Navitimer stainless steel wristwatch, with round-button chronograph, registers, telemeter and slide-rule. c1966 ☆☆☆

▲ A Swiss Breitling 'Long Playing' gold-plated and stainless steel wristwatch, with tonneau-shaped water-resistant case, round-button chronograph, registers and tachometer. c1968 ☆☆

▶ A 1960s Swiss Bueche-Girod 18ct white gold wristwatch, the case in the form of a Volvo car radiator grille, with centre-seconds and date function. ☆☆☆

SWISS MADE

◀ A 1960s Pierre Cardin gentleman's wristwatch, with silvered dial, simple markers and hands, brushed stainless steel case, and Jaeger 17-jewel movement.
☆☆

◀ An English Cartier 'Baignoire Allongèe' 18ct white gold oversized wristwatch, London hallmarks for 1969, the strap with 18ct yellow gold Cartier deployant clasp.
☆☆☆☆☆☆

"Time does not change us. It just unfolds us."

MAX FRISCH

◀ *A French Cartier 18ct gold wristwatch, with back-winding movement by European Watch and Clock Co. Inc, the strap with 18ct pink gold deployant clasp. c1960* ✩✩✩

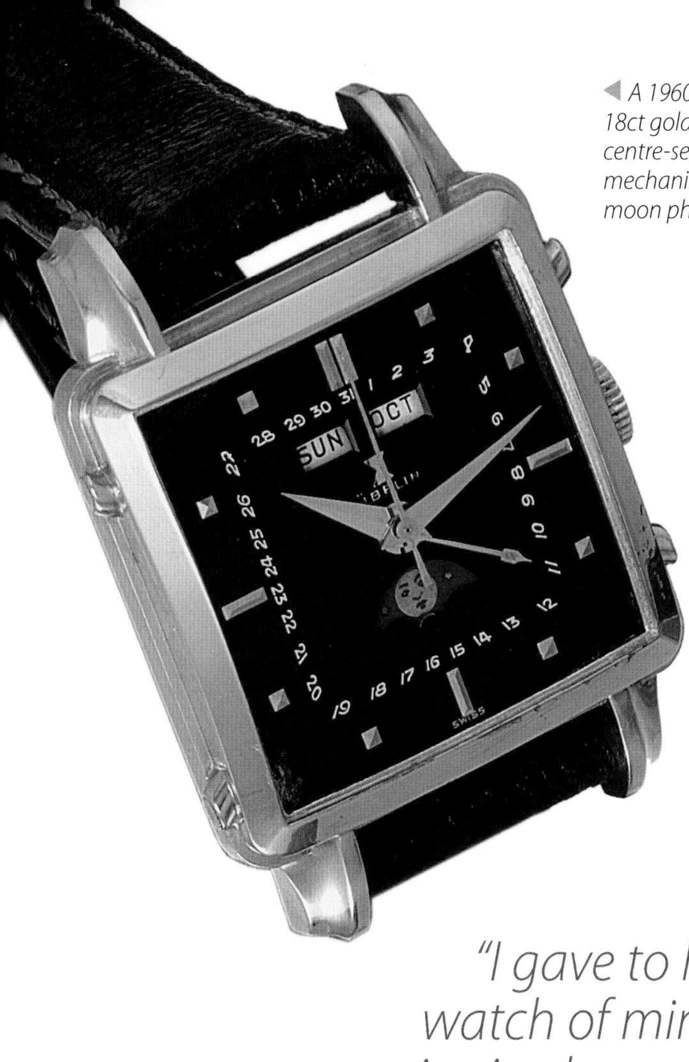

◀ A 1960s Swiss E. Gübelin 18ct gold wristwatch, with centre-seconds, self-winding mechanism, triple-date and moon phases. ☆☆☆

"I gave to Hope a watch of mine; but he An Anchor gave to me."

GEORGE HERBERT

▶ *An American Hamilton Ventura 14ct gold wristwatch, with triangular asymmetric case, centre-seconds and electronically-driven balance. c1960* ☆☆☆

◄ ▶ *A late 1960s Hamilton 'Self-winding' automatic gentleman's wristwatch, no. 941572, with date, 10K gold-filled case, and Swiss-made movement with full rotor.* ☆

▲ *A 1960s Swiss Jaeger-LeCoultre 'Master Mariner' stainless steel wristwatch, with date function, centre-seconds, self-winding mechanism and water-resistant case.* ☆☆

◀ A 1960s Swiss Jaeger-LeCoultre 14ct gold wristwatch, for the American market, the case with engine-turned 'sunray' decoration. ☆☆

194

◀ A 1960s Swiss Jaeger-LeCoultre 'Memovox Speed Beat' stainless steel wristwatch, with water-resistant case, self-winding mechanism, mechanical alarm, date and two crowns. ☆ ☆

"Doing a thing well is often a waste of time."

ROBERT BYRNE

▶ A 1960s Jules Jurgensen automatic gentleman's wristwatch, with large brushed stainless steel case, azure-blue dial, and Jules Jurgensen 21-jewel movement. ☆

▶ A late 1960s Longines 'Comet' wristwatch, with stainless steel cushion-shaped case, 17-jewel manual-wind movement, red and black direct-read mystery dial with rare two-disc arrow pointing minute hand. ☆☆

◀ A 1960s Omega 'Constellation' gentleman's wristwatch, with stainless steel case with 'Observatory' back, and Omega Caliber 561 24-jewel movement with five adjustments. ☆

Omega Speedmaster

One of Omega's most famous ranges, the Speedmaster, was created in 1957. These early models have a hand-wound chronograph movement and a rounded case style. Later models, such as Speedmaster MK II, have a larger case to house the automatic movement. The case was made from just two pieces, which provided better water-resistance, with fewer case-parts to be sealed. Later models also have the tachometer scale beneath the glass, protecting it from damage, whereas on early models the scale was fitted on the outer case bezel, making it very easy to mark.

In 1961, the National Air Space Administration (NASA) purchased two of each of five chronographs of different brands, including the Omega Speedmaster to ascertain their suitability for space travel. The watches were thoroughly subjected to high temperature, low temperature, temperate pressure, relative humidity, oxygen atmosphere, vibration and acoustic noise. The Speedmaster proved the most reliable and so it was chosen as NASA's official watch in 1965. In 1969, the Speedmaster made six round-trips to the moon with Neil Armstrong.

Omega has produced a number of special pieces, including the Speedmaster 125, to celebrate the company's 125th anniversary.

◀ *A Swiss Omega stainless steel Speedmaster Professional wristwatch, with water-resistant case, round-button chronograph, registers and tachometer, with stainless steel Omega link bracelet. c1962* ☆☆☆☆

> *"Watches are a confidence trick invented by the Swiss."*
>
> CHIUN, *RENO WILLIAMS*

◀ *A Swiss Omega Speedmaster 'Moonwatch' stainless steel wristwatch, with water-resistant case, round-button chronograph, registers and tachometer. 1966*
☆☆☆

▲ A Swiss Patek Philippe & Cie
prototype asymmetric
18ct gold wristwatch, designed
by Gilbert Albert. 1960
☆☆☆☆☆

◀ A Swiss Patek
Philippe 18ct gold
wristwatch,
with integral
linen-textured
18ct gold bracelet.
c1968 ☆☆☆

◀ A Swiss Patek
Philippe & Cie
unusual 18ct gold
wristwatch, the
strap with
18ct gold buckle.
1962 ☆☆☆

Piaget

In 1874, Georges Edouard Piaget set up a workshop making movements for watch companies in the Swiss village of La Cote-aux-Fées. His company remains there today but is now renowned for its high quality watches as well as its movements.

Piaget continued to supply movements to other companies until 1943 when the production of watches under the Piaget name began. These are handmade in 18ct gold or platinum and are renowned for their technical and design innovation.

In 1957 Piaget developed the Calibre 9P, a thin, manually-wound watch. The Calibre 12P superceded this in 1960 and, at a mere 2.3mm thick, was the slimmest self-winding watch in the world.

Also typical of the company's work are Piaget's intricate coin, ring, cufflink and brooch watches. The coin watches, for example, consist of a coin-shaped case opened by means of a concealed catch in the milled edge to reveal a watch attached to the centre of the coin by a hinge. They are usually signed on the interior of the coin and on the watch itself. Watches such as these are only possible thanks to the ultra-slim movements Piaget has developed.

From 1964 Piaget began to set watch faces with precious stones: lapis lazuli, onyx, tiger's eye and turquoise being examples.

▶ *A Swiss Piaget 18ct white gold bracelet wristwatch, the case and integral bracelet with hammered decoration and set with a single brilliant-cut diamond. c1968*
☆☆☆☆☆

◀ A 1960s Rolex gentleman's gold wristwatch, the champagne-coloured dial with gold baton numerals and hands, stamped "ROLEX PERPETUAL, OFFICIALLY CERTIFIED CHRONOMETER", numbered to reverse 2241, also stamped with French control marks, fitted to a tan leather strap. ☆☆

◀ A Rolex Oyster Perpetual 'Explorer' stainless steel chronometer wristwatch, with 'Tropical' dial, centre-seconds, water-resistant case and self-winding mechanism, the strap with stainless steel Rolex buckle. 1962 ☆☆☆

208

◀ A Swiss Rolex Oyster 'Dayton' Cosmograph 18ct gold wristwatch, known as the 'Paul Newman' model, with tonneau-shaped water-resistant case, round-button chronograph, registers, anti-reflective black bezel with tachometer graduated to 200uph, with 18ct gold Rolex Oyster riveted bracelet. 1969 ☆☆☆☆☆

▶ A Swiss Tudor 'Submariner' stainless steel diver's wristwatch, made by Rolex, with centre-seconds, self-winding mechanism and water-resistant case to 200m, the strap with stainless steel Rolex buckle. c1967 ☆☆☆

▲ *A 1960s Swiss Universal 'Polerouter' large stainless steel wristwatch, with self-winding mechanism and water-resistant case.* ☆☆☆

▶ *A 1960s Swiss Vacheron & Constantin 18ct pink gold wristwatch, with very thin case.* ☆☆☆

211

► *A Swiss Vacheron & Constantin 18ct gold wristwatch, with centre-seconds, alarm, date, two crowns and hooded lugs, the strap with gold Vacheron buckle. 1966*
☆☆☆☆☆

▶ A 1960s Swiss Zodiac 'Seawolf' automatic diver's wristwatch, in sealed case, with date and two-tone high florescent bezel and dial chapter-ring. ☆

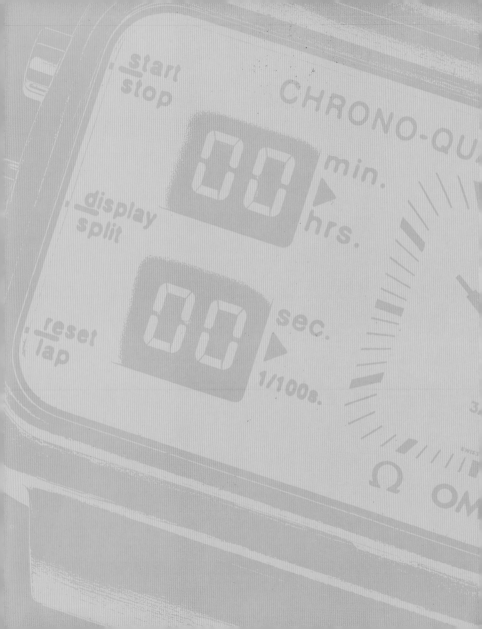

1970s

Watchmakers used the new quartz movements to produce bulky watches with the latest liquid crystal displays or light-emitting diodes. However, a demand for more comfortable and stylish watches soon saw a return to more traditional forms. The first designer watches, from fashion houses such as Chanel and Dior, were made in the 1970s, often by Swiss firms.

▶ An English Cartier 18ct gold large wristwatch, with two straps, each with an 18ct gold buckle, with London hallmarks for 1970-71. ☆☆☆☆☆

"I must start wearing a watch. I never have you know."

MARGO CHANNING,
ALL ABOUT EVE

▲ A Cartier 'Parallèlogramme' 18ct white gold wristwatch, with asymmetric case, the strap with 18ct white and yellow gold Cartier buckle, London import marks for 1973.
☆☆☆☆☆

▶ A 1970s Swiss Gübelin 'G Quartz' stainless steel quartz wristwatch, with date-funtion and stainless steel integral bangle bracelet. ☆

▶ A 1970s Swiss Gruen gentleman's wristwatch, with 16ct gold-plated case with stainless steel back, silvered dial, date and 17-jewel movement. ☆

◄ A Pulsar stainless steel LED quartz wristwatch, made by the Hamilton Watch Co., new-old-stock, with cushion-shaped water-resistant case, and integral, articulated stainless steel Pulsar bracelet. c1972 ☆☆

▲ A 1970s Swiss Heuer 'Autavia' stainless steel wristwatch, with tonneau-shaped water-resistant case, self-winding mechanism, round-button chronograph, registers, tachometer and date-funtion. ☆☆

▲ *A 1970s Swiss Heuer 'Calculator' stainless steel oversized chronograph wristwatch, with tonneau-shaped water-resistant case, round-button chronograph, registers, date-function and calculator, the strap with stainless steel Heuer buckle.* ☆☆☆

▲ *A 1970s Swiss Heuer*
'Monaco' stainless steel
wristwatch, with
self-winding mechanism,
round-button
chronograph, register
and date function.
☆☆☆

◀ A rare LeCoultre gentleman's automatic 'Memovox' alarm wristwatch, signed four times, with three-tone blue dial, egg-shaped stainless steel case and 17-jewel LeCoultre 916 movement. The inner disc revolves, with the arrow-head indicating the time the alarm should go off. The unusual shape is typical of this short period, and was deemed avant garde at the time, as well as being expensive. HPG stands for 'High Precision Guaranteed', further denoting its expense at the time. 1969-72 ☆☆

▶ A 1970s Swiss Jaeger-LeCoultre mystery dial 18ct gold wristwatch, the tonneau-shaped case wtih hooded lugs. ☆☆☆

226

Longines

Longines is the world's oldest registered brand name in watch-making, maintaining twin values of 'science and elegance' for over a hundred years. The company are famous for their ultra-thin watches and their extremely precise time keeping: a quality utilised by the Olympic Games and the Ferrari Formula 1 racing team. Albert Einstein carried a Longines pocket watch.

The first Longines factory was built in 1866 by Ernest Francillon on the right bank of the Suze river, near a place called Les Longines. He registered the brand name and winged-hourglass logo in 1880. Longines was the first company to produce wristwatches by largely mechanical means in 1905. As early as 1912, they eschewed the typical round form for rectangular and square-shaped models. This evolved into the range of Art Deco watches Longines produced in the 1920s and '30s and other elegant geometric designs.

Longines is also famous for its 'Aviator' watches and has been the official supplier to the International Aeronautics Federatio (IAF) since 1919. In 1927, Charles A. Lindbergh made the first solo and non-stop transatlantic flight from New York to Paris timed by Longines. Lindberg later designed a pilot watch to help with air navigation, which is still produced by the company.

◀ *A 1970s Longines automatic gentleman's wristwatch, signed four times on the movement, dial, case and crown, with blue dial and date window, and pillow-shaped stainless steel case.* ☆

▶ *A 1970s Swiss Moeris 'James Bond 007' stainless steel wristwatch, with octagonal water-resistant case, centre-seconds and self-winding mechanism.*
✩✩✩

◀ *A 1970s Swiss Movado 18ct white gold wristwatch, with two time-zones and two movements, with an integral, textured 18ct gold bracelet.* ☆☆☆

▶ *A limited edition Swiss Omega Speedmaster 125 stainless steel chronometer wristwatch, from an edition of 2,000 to celebrate the 125th anniversary of Omega, with tonneau-shaped water-resistant case, date-function, round-button chronograph, 12-hour register, central minute-counter, tachometer and 24-hour night/day indicator, and with stainless steel articulated Omega bracelet with deployant clasp. 1973* ☆☆☆

> "The days of the digital watch are numbered."

TOM STOPPARD

▶ A Swiss Omega
'Dynamic' stainless steel
automatic wristwatch,
with water-resistant case,
centre-seconds display,
and date-function, the
strap with stainless steel
Omega buckle. c1973
☆☆☆

Digital watches

Perhaps surprisingly, a form of digital timekeeping dates back almost 200 years. The first wristwatches that could be termed 'digital' were made in the 1930s, primarily by lesser-known companies such as the Awoner Watch Co. in Switzerland. These watches used various dials – rather than the traditional face and hands – including an hour dial attached to a complicated mechanism that jumped after 59 minutes – visible through apertures in a chrome-plated, silver or gold case.

The LED (light-emitting diode) was invented in the 1960s, and this made possible what we would recognise as a digital watch – a watch with an electronic screen. The first digital watch without any moving parts was the Pulsar: developed jointly by Hamilton Watch Company and Electro-Data and made in 1970. James Bond could be seen wearing a Pulsar on his wrist in 'Live and Let Die' (1973).

Unfortunately, the LED movements consumed a lot of power and even with the display lit for only 1¼ seconds at a time, an LED watch needed two batteries the size of a hearing aid to run for just six months.

The introduction of the LCD (liquid crystal display) screen in the mid-1970s made LED displays redundant. The new displays always remained visible, and consumed far less power. The watches were also slimmer and more affordable.

Digital watches remained popular until the 1990s when analogue watches returned to favour.

◀ *A Swiss Omega 'Time Computer' gold-capped stainless steel digital-display wristwatch, with red LED display for the time and date and matching articulated bar-link bracelet with deployant clasp. c1975* ☆☆☆

◀ A 1970s Swiss Omega 'Electronic' stainless steel chronometer wristwatch, with tonneau-shaped water-resistant case, centre-seconds and date-function, with stainless steel Omega bracelet and deployant clasp. ☆☆

▶ A Swiss Omega 'Seamaster' Chrono-Quartz 32KHz stainless steel oversized wristwatch, with two LCD digital displays for the round-button chronograph, together with an analogue display for the time-function, with integral stainless steel Omega bar bracelet and deployant clasp. c1977 ☆☆☆

235

▶ *A Swiss Patek Philippe & Cie 18ct gold wristwatch, with integral 18ct gold Patek cylindrical-link bracelet. 1976 ☆☆☆*

PATEK PHILIPPE
GENÈVE

SWISS

◄ A 1970s Swiss Piaget 18ct gold wristwatch, with dual time-zones and two movements, the strap with 18ct gold Piaget buckle. ☆☆☆

▶ *A 1970s Swiss Piaget 18ct white gold wristwatch, with thin, cushion-shaped case.*
☆☆

"[Earth's] ape-descended life forms are so amazingly primitive that they still think digital watches are a pretty neat idea."

DOUGLAS ADAMS

▶ *A 1970s Rolex 'Cellini' 18ct gold left-handed wristwatch, with asymmetric square case and integrated 18ct gold Rolex cylindrical-link bracelet.* ☆☆☆

▶ A 1970s Swiss Vacheron & Constantin Automatic 18ct gold wristwatch, the tonneau-shaped case with lapis lazuli dial, self-winding mechanism, integral, textured 18ct gold Vacheron bracelet. ☆☆☆

▶ A Swiss Vacheron & Constantin 18ct gold wristwatch, with dual time-zone display and two movements, the strap with 18ct gold Vacheron & Constantin buckle. 1978 ☆☆☆☆

"Love vanquishes time. To lovers, a moment can be eternity, eternity can be the tick of a clock."

MARY PARRISH

1980s

Novel or unusual designs, as much as technical innovation, fuelled the watch industry throughout the 1980s. Tissot's Rock Watch and Corum's Météorite – each one made from a piece of Swiss granite or slice of meteorite respectively – were guaranteed to be unique. The launch of Swatch meant a new type of watch appeared, appealing to the younger generation, or simply the young at heart.

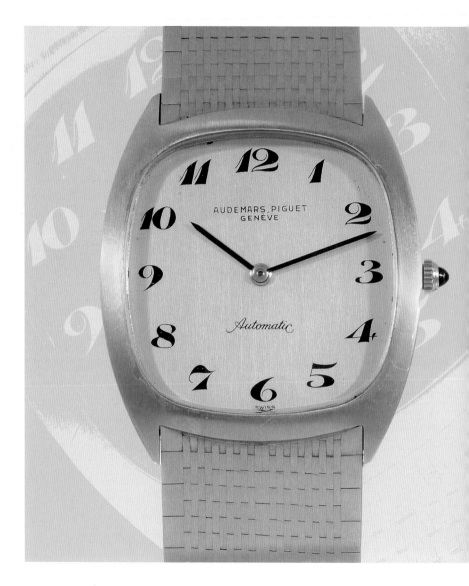

Audemars Piguet

Along with Patek Philippe and Vacheron-Constantin, Audemars Piguet is considered to be one of the 'big-three': producing some of the finest watches in the world. It currently employs 700 people worldwide, who create more than 24,000 watches, by hand, every year.

The company is the product of a partnership between Jules Audemars and Edward-August Piguet. They founded Audemars Piguet et Cie shortly after their first meeting in 1875, when Piguet was just 21. The Audemars Piguet trademark was registered in 1882 and it was another seven years before the company was officially founded, when it successfully became the third largest employer for watch manufacturing in the Canton of Vaud. Following the official founding in 1889 a new branch office was built in Geneva. The partners decided to produce all of their components and assemble the watches in-house, allowing strict quality control.

In 1892, Audemars Piguet developed and produced the first minute-repeater wristwatch. Twenty three years later, they set a world record that remains unmatched to this day, by creating the smallest five-minute-repeater movement of all time.

Perhaps the most famous Audemar Piguet watch, the Royal Oak (with its instantly recognisable guilloché dial, octagonal bezel and integrated bracelet) was created in 1972. It was the first high-end steel sports watch and completely overturned the existing codes of Haute Horlogerie with its dedication to technical sophistication and ultimate performance and resistance. For the company's 30th anniversary the watch was re-launched in titanium and 602 alacrite.

◀ *A 1980s Swiss Audemars Piguet 18ct white gold automatic wristwatch, with 18ct white gold bracelet.* ☆☆☆

"There is never enough time, unless you're serving it."

MALCOLM FORBES

▶ *A Swiss Audemars Piguet 'Tourbillon Automatique' 18ct gold wristwatch, with visible one-minute tourbillon regulator and with 18ct gold Audemars Piguet double-deployant clasp. c1986* ☆☆☆☆

◀ *A 1980s Swiss Breguet 'Serpentine' 18ct gold wristwatch, retailed by Tiffany & Co., with triple date-function, moon phases and age of the moon, the strap with 18ct gold Breguet buckle and setting pin on a chain.* ☆☆☆☆☆

▶ A Swiss Cartier Pasha
18ct gold wristwatch, with
water-resistant case,
centre-seconds,
date-function and
self-winding mechanism,
the strap with 18ct gold
Cartier deployant clasp. 1989
☆☆☆

◀ A limited series
Swiss Cartier
'Ferrari F40' 18ct gold
chronograph
wristwatch, from a
series of 140
commissioned by Enzo
Ferrari to commemorate his
last project, the F40, with
water-resistant case,
self-winding mechanism,
hexagonal-button
chronograph, registers,
tachometer and
date-function, the strap
with stainless steel and gold
Ferrari deployant clasp, never
commercially sold. 1986
☆☆☆☆

Limited Edition Watches

To be considered a limited edition, a watch – or any other collectable – should be made in a limited number and for a limited period. Usually, each piece will have been numbered (this may be engraved on the case) and will have been sold with a certificate of authenticity. It is important that all paperwork and packaging are retained or the value will fall considerably.

There may also be variations within the limited edition to attract collectors of different levels. For example, The International Watch Company's limited edition 'Portugieser 2000' which was produced in 1,000 steel, 750 rose gold and 250 platinum models. The first 100 in the series were sold as boxed sets, each one with a companion steel, gold and platinum watch with the same edition number on each watch. All the watches had the limited edition number engraved on the case. This watch is also available as a standard model which is not limited to an edition.

Another maker who has created limited edition watches is Swatch, which commissions designers such as Vivienne Westwood and Alessandro Mendini, or makes watches to commemorate events such as the Olympics. Patek Philippe created several limited editions to celebrate its 150th anniversary in 1989, including the 'Calibre 89' of which only three examples were made: in yellow, white and pink gold. The yellow gold example sold for £1 million ($2 million).

◀ *A limited edition Swiss International Watch Co. 'Fliegerchronograph' 18ct gold quartz wristwatch, from an edition of 120 to celebrate the 120th anniversary of IWC, with water-resistant case, round-button chronograph, registers and date-function, the strap with gold-plated IWC buckle. 1988 ☆☆☆*

▶ *A Swiss Jaeger-LeCoultre Series Unique 18ct gold wristwatch, with triple-date and moon phases, with integral 18ct gold bracelet. 1983*
✩✩✩

◀ A limited edition Swiss Movado ' Andy Warhol Times/5' black stainless steel wristwatch, from an edition of 250, with five dials representing five different views of New York for five different time-zones. 1988 ☆☆☆

"I don't wear a watch. How do I know the time? I find that someone will always tell me"

CARRIE BRADSHAW, *SEX AND THE CITY*

◀ A Swiss Omega 'Sensor' gold-plated stainless steel LCD quartz wristwatch, with chronograph, day, date, alarm, agenda and second time-zone, with integral gold-plated stainless steel Omega bracelet. c1980 ☆☆☆

▶ A Swiss Omega
'La Magique' 18ct gold
mystery quartz wristwatch,
with transparent dial centre
composed of two revolving
sapphire-coloured discs in a
very slim case, the strap
with 18ct gold Omega
buckle. c1981 ☆☆☆

▶ A Swiss Omega 18ct gold quartz wristwatch, with ultra-slim case, the integral 18ct gold Omega bracelet with concealed deployant clasp. c1981 ✩✩✩

▶ A Swiss Omega 'De Ville' stainless steel wristwatch, with rectangular blue dial, the strap with stainless steel Omega buckle. c1981 ✩✩

◀ *A limited production Swiss Patek Philippe & Cie 18ct gold wristwatch, with self-winding mechanism, perpetual calendar, moon phases and Roman numerals for the leap year indication, the strap with 18ct gold Patek Philippe buckle. 1983* ☆☆☆☆☆☆

▲ *A Swiss Patek Philippe & Cie 'Nautilus' stainless steel mid-sized quartz wristwatch, with water-resistant case, centre-seconds and date-function, with stainless steel Patek Philippe bracelet. 1987* ☆☆☆

▲ A Swiss Rolex Oyster Perpetual Date 'Sea-Dweller 200' stainless steel diver's chronometer wristwatch, with water-resistant case, centre-seconds, self-winding mechanism, helium escape valve and date-function, with a stainless steel Oyster Fliplock bracelet. 1982
☆☆☆☆

◄ A Swiss Rolex Oyster Cosmograph 'Daytona' stainless steel wristwatch, with water-resistant case, black bezel, round-button chronograph, registers and tachometer, with stainless steel Rolex Oyster bracelet. 1984 ☆☆☆☆☆

1990s

Despite continuing developments in technology, and the growth of the quartz watch market, the demand for mechanical watches grew into a collector's market. The desire for novelty inspired watchmakers to create ever more complicated and unusual models to appeal to a growing number of collectors.

▶ *A limited edition 1990s Swiss Blancpain '1735 Grande Complication' platinum large astronomic wristwatch, from an edition of 30 which started production in 1991, with self-winding mechanism, one-minute tourbillon regulator, round-button co-axial split-seconds chronograph, register, perpetual calendar, moon phases and moon age, the strap with platinum Blancpain deployant clasp.* ☆☆☆☆☆☆

▼ A limited edition French Cartier 'Parallélogramme' asymmetric 18ct gold wristwatch, from an edition of 300, based on the 1930s design, the strap with 18ct pink gold Cartier deployant clasp. 1996 ☆☆☆

"Did you ever ask a lawyer the time of day? He told you how to make a watch, didn't he?"

HAL PHILLIP WALKER, *NASHVILLE*

▶ *A 1990s Swiss Jaeger-LeCoultre 'Geographique' 18ct yellow gold wristwatch, with world time, centre-seconds, self-winding, water-resistant, 45-hour power reserve, day and night indication, with 18ct yellow gold Jaeger-LeCoultre buckle.*
☆☆☆☆

◀ *A Swiss Girard-Perregaux 'Richeville Tourbillon' 18ct white gold wristwatch, with tonneau-shaped water-resistant case and one-minute tourbillon regulator, the strap with 18ct white gold Girard-Perregaux buckle. 1994* ☆☆☆☆☆

Jaeger-LeCoultre

The luxury watch and clock manufacturer, Jaeger-LeCoultre is based in the remote village of Le Sentier in Switzerland. It was founded in 1833 by Antoine LeCoultre who specialised in instruments and geared mechanisms. As his business grew, he began to produce watch-movement blanks and ended up with 125 different types. Both sons joined him in the company, which then began to produce minute-repeaters, chronographs and calendar watch-movements to be sold to other watch companies who would add their names to the finished pieces.

Jacques-David, grandson of Antoine, developed a business relationship with Parisian watch-maker, Edmond Jaeger after LeCoultre successfully manufactured ultra-thin calibres of Jaeger's designs in 1903. From 1930, they produced the Atmos clock – which gets the energy it needs from small atmospheric changes and therefore never needs to be wound – and, from 1931, the Reverso watch. The firm became officially known as Jaeger-LeCoultre in 1938, although the name LeCoultre was still used in the USA until the early 1970s.

Jaeger-LeCoultre is now owned by the Richemont group who have expanded the factory and now produce movements for their own watches, rather than other companies.

◀ *A 1990s Swiss Jaeger-LeCoultre Reverso 'Memory' 18ct gold and stainless steel reversible wristwatch, with two dials, permanent minute-register and fly-back mechanism, 50-hours autonomy, with 18ct gold and stainless steel Jaeger-LeCoultre 'bracelet a mailles' and deployant clasp.* ☆☆☆

"Ha, ha! keep time: how sour sweet music is, When time is broke and no proportion kept!"

WILLIAM SHAKESPEARE

◀ A 1990s Swiss Jean d'Eve 'Samara' stainless steel wristwatch, with battery-free quartz movement, visible rotor and date, the strap with stainless steel Jean d'Eve buckle. ☆☆

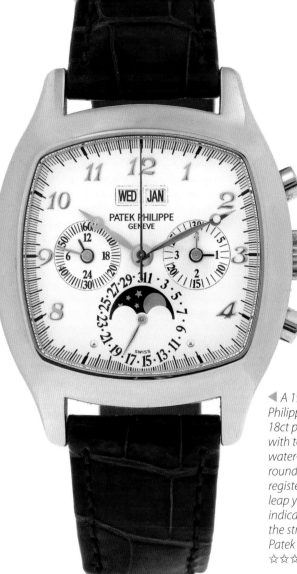

◀ A 1990s Swiss Patek Philippe & Cie 'TV Watch' 18ct pink gold wristwatch, with tonneau-shaped, water-resistant case, round-button chronograph, register, perpetual calendar, leap year and 24-hour indication and moon phases, the strap with 18ct pink gold Patek Philippe buckle.
☆☆☆☆☆☆

▼ A 1990s Swiss Piaget 18ct white gold wristwatch, with thin square case, the strap with 18ct white gold Piaget buckle. ✩✩✩

◀ A limited edition Swiss Patek Philippe 'Pagoda' 18ct white gold chronometer wristwatch, from an edition of 250 for the inauguration of the new Patek Philippe Manufactory in Geneva, the design based on Patek's 1940s 'Eiffel Tower' design, the strap with 18ct white gold Patek Philippe buckle. 1997 ✩✩✩✩✩✩

◀ A Swiss Rolex Oyster Perpetual Date Explorer II stainless steel chronometer wristwatch, with rare ivory dial, two time-zones, centre-seconds, self-winding mechanism, water-resistant case, date function, independently adjustable 12-hour hand, with a stainless steel Oyster bracelet. 1991
☆☆☆☆

"All that really belongs to us is time; even he who has nothing else has that."

BALTASAR GRACIAN

◀ *A limited edition Swiss Alain Silberstein 'Cyclope' stainless steel wristwatch, from an edition of 500, with wandering jump-hours, centre-seconds, self-winding mechanism and water-resistant case. 1995* ☆☆☆

Swatch

The Swiss watch industry struggled through the 1970s. The workforce of over 100,000 was cut by half due to competition from digital watches made by Japanese companies like Sieko. The launch of the Swatch watch in 1983 finally revitalised interest in analogue watches.

A contraction of 'Second Watch', the Swatch was marketed as a casual, fun, and relatively disposable accessory. The quartz watch was redesigned for manufacturing efficiency and fewer parts. The movement was built into the case and without a back to open this made the Swatch waterproof as well as light. Famous designers, such as Vivienne Westwood, were employed to design limited production runs.

The Swatch was so successful that, by 1992, the 100 millionth watch had been produced. This same year Swatch released the Chandelier watch for Christmas in London. On the opening day over 400 people queued up to buy the watch at 10 o'clock and by 3 o'clock 1,000 had been sold.

The Swatch group is now the world's largest watch company and includes Breguet, Omega, Longines, Tissot, Calvin Klein and Blancpain. Currently, there are three families under the Swatch brand: Swatch Original (plastic cased), Swatch Irony (metal cased) and Swatch Skin (ultra thin).

◀ *A limited edition Swiss Swatch 'Trésor Magique' platinum wristwatch, from an edition of 12,999, with tonneau-shaped water-resistant case, centre-seconds, self-winding mechanism, the strap with a stainless steel Swatch buckle. The 'Trésor Magique' was the only watch to be made of precious metal by Swatch. 1993* ☆☆☆

▲ A late 1990s Swiss Tag Heuer
'S/EL Chrono' stainless steel wristwatch,
with water-resistant case, self-winding
mechanism, round-button chronograph,
registers, date-function and tachometer,
with stainless steel Tag Heuer link bracelet
with deployant clasp. ☆☆

"Reminds me of a guy I know who got a nice cushy job in a watch factory... He stands about all day and makes faces."

BERT, *MARY POPPINS*

▶ *A 1990s Swiss Universal 'Compax' manual-wind chronograph gentleman's wristwatch, with white dial with three registers, sapphire crystal, signed seven times, and with signed Universal Geneve 31-jewel movement.* ☆☆

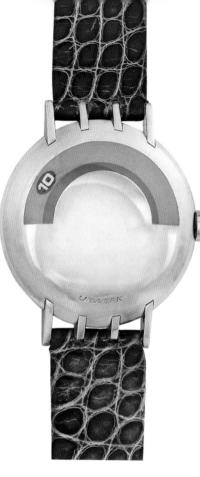

"Dictionaries are like watches; the worst is better than none, and the best cannot be expected to go quite true."

SAMUEL JOHNSON

▲ A late 1990s Swiss Unwerk 'Nightwatch' stainless steel wristwatch, the leather strap with matching Unwerk buckle.
☆☆☆☆

▶ *A 1990s Swiss Vacheron-Constantin 'Mercator Orient & Occident' 18ct gold wristwatch, the case water-resistant to 30 meters, with 22ct gold dial representing the continents of Europe, Africa, Australia and Asia, double-sector graduated for 12 hours and 60 minutes with retrograde hands, the strap with 18ct gold Vacheron-Constantin deployant clasp.*
☆☆☆☆

2000s

The market for luxury watches has been driven by the increasing wealth around the globe. Watches are now being seen as a fashion accessory, rather than simply a means of telling the time, and this has fuelled sales, even while the cost of high-end watches has increased. Switzerland continues to be the largest manufacturer of watches in terms of value, no doubt thanks to the unwavering high quality of its work.

◀ A Swiss Audemars Piguet 'Millenary' automatic 18ct white gold wristwatch, with centre-seconds, water-resistant case and date function, the strap with 18ct white gold Audemars deployant clasp. 2006 ☆☆☆☆

◀ A limited edition Swiss Breguet Grand Complication 'Tourbillon 1801-2001' 18ct white gold and diamond wristwatch, from an edition of 28 to commemorate the 200th anniversary of the invention of the tourbillon regulating device by Abraham-Louis Breguet, the half-hunter case pave-set with 402 brilliant-cut diamonds with visible one-minute tourbillon regulator and an 18K white gold Breguet deployant clasp. 2001 ☆☆☆☆☆☆

"Man is a watch, wound up at first, but never Wound up again"

ROBERT HERRICK

▶ *A limited production French Cartier Tortue minute-repeating 18ct white gold wristwatch, the strap with 18ct white gold Cartier deployant clasp. c2000* ☆☆☆☆☆

◀ *A Swiss Chanel J12 automatic black ceramic and stainless steel wristwatch, with centre-seconds, self-winding mechanism and tonneau-shaped water-resistant case, the strap with stainless steel Chanel deployant clasp. c2000* ☆☆☆

▶ A limited edition Swiss Girard-Perregaux 'Ferrari' titanium chronograph wristwatch, from an edition of 100 commemorating the Scuderia Ferrari between 1929-1999, with self-winding mechanism, water-resistant case, 1/8 seconds round-button split-seconds 'foudroyante' chronograph, registers and tachometer, with titanium Girard-Perregaux link bracelet with double deployant clasp. 2000
☆☆☆

◀ A limited edition Swiss Corum 'Bubble – Royal Flush' stainless steel wristwatch, the official watch of the World Series of Poker, with self-winding mechanism, water-resistant case, centre-seconds and thick-domed crystal creating a lens-effect, the strap with stainless steel Corum deployant clasp. 2006
☆☆☆

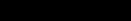

JAMES BOND. MY CHOICE.

**AVAILABLE AT
OMEGA BOUTIQUES:**

12 OLD BOND STREET
LONDON

ROYAL EXCHANGE
LONDON

TERMINAL 1
HEATHROW AIRPORT

AND AT FINE JEWELLERS AND
WATCH SPECIALISTS NATIONWIDE.

Limited edition

Ω
OMEGA

James Bond's Watches

Watches in films are usually only glimpsed beneath shirt cuffs, but James Bond's watches have a much more important role to play. Enhanced by 'Q' they become crucial tools enabling the hero to escape from mortal danger.

Bond's watch was identified by Ian Fleming as a Rolex Oyster Perpetual Chronometer in *On Her Majesty's Secret Service*, in which he uses his watch as an improvised knuckleduster. When Sean Connery appeared in the first James Bond film, *Dr No*, he, too, wore a Rolex: the Submariner. Roger Moore also wore a Submariner and the early models are now so closely associated with the films that they are known as 'James Bond watches'.

Moore's Rolex was retired in favour of a Seiko in *The Spy Who Loved Me*. With the arrival of Pierce Brosnan in *Goldeneye*, the watch became an Omega Seamaster. Daniel Craig's Bond also wears a Seamaster in both *Casino Royale* and *Quantum of Solace*. The company produced a limited edition of the Seamaster (10,007 pieces) for the 40th anniversary of James Bond.

◀ *The Omega Seamaster: James Bond's choice – wearing one can make anyone feel like a secret agent.*

◀ The Omega 'Seamaster' Professional stainless steel diver's wristwatch worn by Pierce Brosnan as James Bond during the filming of 'Tomorrow Never Dies' in 1996-97, with self-winding mechanism, water-resistant case, centre-seconds, date-function, blue bezel for the decompression times, stainless steel Omega brick-link bracelet with deployant clasp, case back engraved 'worn by James Bond – 1997 – Tomorrow Never Dies'.
☆☆☆☆☆

◀ The Omega 'Seamaster' Professional 'Planet Ocean' stainless steel diver's wristwatch worn by Daniel Craig as James Bond during the filming of 'Casino Royale' in 2005-06, with self-winding mechanism, water-resistant case, centre-seconds, date-function, revolving black bezel for the decompression times, the rubber strap with a stainless steel Omega buckle.
☆☆☆☆☆

▲ A Swiss Patek Philippe 18ct white gold 'Celestial Wristwatch', with water-resistant case, self-winding mechanism, water-resistant, mean solar time indication, nocturnal sky chart of the Northern Hemisphere, moon phases and moon orbit and time of the meridian passage of Sirius and moon, the strap with 18ct white gold Patek Philippe buckle. c2002 ☆☆☆☆☆☆

▶ A Swiss Rolex Oyster Perpetual 'Daytona' steel and 18ct gold wristwatch, with water-resistant case, self-winding mechanism, round-button chronograph, registers and tachometer, with stainless steel and 18ct gold Rolex Oysterlock bracelet. 2006
☆☆☆☆

▶ *A limited edition Swiss Swatch 'Diaphane One' translucent plastic and aluminium wristwatch, from an edition of 2,222, with water-resistant case, set with diamond, sapphire and rubies and 30-minute revolving escapement, the strap with aluminium Swatch buckle. 2001* ☆☆☆

▲ *A Swiss Vacheron-Constantin 'Malte Tonneau Tourbillon' 18ct pink gold wristwatch, with visible one-minute tourbillon regulator, 42-hour power-reserve and date-function, the dial with Maltese cross, the regulator with Maltese cross-shaped steel cage. 2001*
☆☆☆☆☆

Acknowledgements

Antiquorum

**2, rue du Mont-Blanc
CH 1211 Geneva 1
Tel: +41 (0)22 909 28 50
Fax: +41 (0)22 909 28 59**

**595 Madison Ave., Fifth
Floor, New York,
NY 10022
Tel: +1 212 750 1103
Fax: +1 212 750 6127**

**Piazza Duomo, 21
20121 Milano
Tel: +39.02.876625
Fax: +39.02.877915**

www.antiquorum.com

10, 11, 13, 15, 18, 19, 20,
21, 23, 24, 25, 27, 30, 31,
32, 33, 34, 35, 40, 41, 42,
43, 44, 45, 46, 47, 48, 49,
51, 52, 53, 54, 55, 56, 57,
58, 59, 60, 61, 64, 65, 67,
68, 77, 79, 80, 81, 82, 83,
85, 86, 87, 88, 89, 90, 91,
92, 93, 94, 95, 96, 97, 98,
99, 100, 104, 107, 109,
110, 114, 115, 117, 119,
122, 124, 125, 126, 127,
128, 129, 130, 132, 133,
134, 135, 141, 142, 152,
153, 157, 158, 166, 167,
168, 169, 170, 172, 173,
174, 176, 177, 180, 181,
182, 183, 184, 185, 187,
188, 189, 190, 192, 193,
194, 198, 200, 201, 202,
203, 205, 206, 208, 209,
210, 211, 212, 216, 217,
219, 220, 221, 222, 223,
225, 228, 229, 230, 231,
232, 234, 235, 236, 237,
238, 239, 240, 241, 244,
246, 247, 248, 249, 250,
252, 253, 254, 255, 256,
257, 258, 259, 260, 261,
264, 265, 266, 267, 268,
270, 271, 272, 273, 274,
275, 276, 278, 280, 281,
284, 285, 286, 287, 288,
289, 292, 293, 294, 295,
296, 297

**Mark Laino
c/o South Street
Antiques Market,
615 South 6th Street,
Philadelphia,
PA 19147-2128 USA**

lecoultre@verizon.net

14, 36, 37, 66, 69, 70, 71,
72, 73, 74, 76, 78, 101,
105, 106, 111, 112, 113,
116, 118, 120, 121, 131,
138, 139, 140, 143, 144,
145, 146, 147, 148, 149,
150, 151, 154, 156, 159,
160, 161, 162, 163, 164,
165, 171, 186, 191, 195,
196, 197, 213, 218, 224,
226, 279

Lyon & Turnbull

**33 Broughton Place,
Edinburgh EH1 3RR
Tel: +44 (0)131 557
8844
Fax: +44 (0)131 557
8668
www.lyonandturnbull.
com**

207

Also

Front cover: Tag Heuer
SA; 39 Octopus
Publishing Group/Robin
Saker;

290, 291 The Advertising
Archive.

The publisher would like
to thank Caroline
Guennelon and her team
at Antiquorum for their
help in researching the
images and captions for
this book.

Museums

BELGIUM
Clock and Watch Museum
Lange schipstraat 13, 2800
Mechelen
www.horlogeriemuseum.be

FRANCE
**Musee International
D'Horlogerie**
48 rue Edouard Cannevel,
F-76 510 Saint-Nicolas
d'Aliermont
www.musee-horlogerie-
aliermont.fr

GERMANY
Deutsches Uhrenmuseum
robert-gerwig-platz 1, d-78120
furtwangen
http://deutsches-
uhrenmuseum.de

SWITZERLAND
Cité du Temps
Pont de la Machine 1, 1204
Genève
www.citedutemps.com

Girard Perregaux
www.girard-perregaux.com

Longines Museum
Les Longines, 2610 St-Imier
www.longines.com

**Museum fur Uhren und
Mechanische Musik**
Staatsstrasse 18, Ch-3653
Oberhofen
www.uhrenmuseum.ch

Musée Audemars Piguet
1348 Le Brassus, Switzerland
www.audemarspiguet.com

**Musée d'Horlogerie du Locle,
Château des Monts**
Rte. des Monts 65, CH-2400
Le Locle
www.mhl-monts.ch

Omega Museum
rue Stämpfli 96, CH-2504
Bienne
www.omega.ch

Patek Philippe Museum
Rue des Vieux-Grenadiers 7,
CH - 1205 Geneva
www.patekmuseum.com

Uhrenmuseum Beyer
Bahnhofstrasse 31, 8001 Zurich
www.beyer-chronometrie.ch

Watchmaking Space
Grand-Rue 2, Case postale 126,
1347 Le Sentier
www.espacehorloger.ch

UK
British Horological Institute
Upton Hall, Upton, Newark
Notts, NG23 5TE
www.bhi.co.uk

British Museum
Great Russell Street, London
WC1B 3DG
www.britishmuseum.org

Clockmakers' Museum
The Clock Room, Guildhall
library, Aldermanbury, London,
EC2P 2EJ
www.clockmakers.org

Fitzwilliam Museum
Trumpington Street,
Cambridge, CB2 1RB
www.fitzmuseum.cam.ac.uk

**Ipswich Museums & Art
galleries**
High Street, Ipswich,
Suffolk. HP1 3QH
http://www.ipswich.gov.uk

Museum of London
London Wall, London,
EC2Y 5HN
www.museumoflondon.org.uk

Museum of the History of Science

Old Ashmolean Building, Broad Street, Oxford, OX1 3AZ

www.mhs.ox.ac.uk

National Maritime Museum

Greenwich, London SE10 9NF

www.nmm.ac.uk

Royal Museum of Scotland

Chambers Street, Edinburgh, EH1 1JF

www.nms.ac.uk

Science Museum

Exhibition Road, London SW7 2DD.

www.sciencemuseum.org.uk

Victoria & Albert Museum

Cromwell Road, London SW7 2 RL

www.vam.ac.uk

Whipple Museum of the History of Science

Free School Lane, Cambridge, CB2 3RH

www.hps.cam.ac.uk/whipple

Willis Museum

Old Town Hall, Market Square, Basingstoke, RG21 1QD

http://www3.hants.gov.uk

World Museum

William Brown Street, Liverpool, L3 8EN

www.liverpoolmuseums.org.uk

USA

Hoffman Clock Museum

121 High Street, Newark, NY

www.hoffmanclockmuseum.org

National Watch & Clock Museum

514 Poplar Street, Columbia, PA

www.nawcc.org

The Museum of Science and Industry

57th Street and Lake Shore Drive, Chicago, IL 60637

www.msichicago.org

Whatcom Museum

121 Prospect Street, Bellingham, WA 98225

http://whatcommuseum.org

Timexpo Museum

175 Union Street, Brass Mill Commons Mall, Waterbury, CT 06706

www.timexpo.com

Index